BIRDS

Explore their extraordinary world

MIRANDA KRESTOVNIKOFF

illustrated by

ANGELA HARDING

BLOOMSBURY
CHILDREN'S BOOKS
NEW YORK LONDON OXFORD NEW DELHI SYDNEY

For Amélie and Oliver
and in memory of those brave and pioneering Victorian women,
Emily Williamson and Eliza Phillips, who were the driving force
behind the creation of the Royal Society for the Protection of Birds
—M. K.

To my father, Stephen Harding
—A. H.

BLOOMSBURY CHILDREN'S BOOKS
Bloomsbury Publishing Inc., part of Bloomsbury Publishing Plc
1385 Broadway, New York, NY 10018

BLOOMSBURY, BLOOMSBURY CHILDREN'S BOOKS, and the Diana logo
are trademarks of Bloomsbury Publishing Plc

First published in Great Britain in February 2020 by Bloomsbury Publishing Plc
Published in the United States of America in April 2021
by Bloomsbury Children's Books

Bloomsbury books may be purchased for business or promotional use. For information on bulk purchases
please contact Macmillan Corporate and Premium Sales Department at specialmarkets@macmillan.com

Library of Congress Cataloging-in-Publication Data
Names: Krestovnikoff, Miranda, author. | Harding, Angela, illustrator.
Title: Birds : explore their extraordinary world / by Miranda Krestovnikoff ;
illustrated by Angela Harding.
Description: New York : Bloomsbury Children's Books, 2021.
Summary: A heavily designed and stunning look at the many birds of the sky—perfect for fans of Botanicum.
Identifiers: LCCN 2020028851 (print) | LCCN 2020028852 (e-book)
ISBN 978-1-5476-0529-3 (hardcover)
ISBN 978-1-5476-0746-4 (e-pub) • ISBN 978-1-5476-0747-1 (e-PDF)
Subjects: LCSH: Birds—Juvenile literature.
Classification: LCC QL676.2 .K74 2021 (print) | LCC QL676.2 (e-book) | DDC 598—dc23
LC record available at https://lccn.loc.gov/2020028851
LC e-book record available at https://lccn.loc.gov/2020028852

Book design by Claire Jones
Typeset in Foundry Wilson
Printed in China by Leo Paper Products, Heshan, Guangdong
2 4 6 8 10 9 7 5 3 1

To find out more about our authors and books visit www.bloomsbury.com and sign up for our newsletters.

CONTENTS

INTRODUCTION

Birds have conquered every continent on Earth, making homes in almost every habitat, from the freezing-cold polar regions to the lush tropics. Whether it's powerful golden eagles swooping down to pounce on their prey, urban pigeons pecking on pavements, or fluttering sparrows in hedgerows, birds can be spotted the world over.

Birds evolved from dinosaurs, but what set them apart was their incredible ability to fly. Unlike reptiles, they had a unique way of escaping hungry predators and moving to new places—flight.

Flight requires a lot of energy, so birds needed to adapt: feathers cover their bodies for warmth and to create streamlined flight, and many birds developed hollow bones to lighten the load and increase efficiency in the air.

Flight gave birds the ability to conquer the skies, some choosing to spend many years on the wing before landing to breed, others undertaking vast migrations to new lands in search of food and warmer climates.

Flight isn't birds' only remarkable feature. They produce some of the most beautiful sounds in nature, and many have astonishingly colorful and elaborate plumage. Sadly, this has often resulted in species becoming endangered due to people's desire to collect and wear their feathers. This is not the only danger these graceful creatures face; while some species thrive in our towns and cities, others are fast disappearing due to loss of habitat as the human population expands.

Now more than ever, we need to ensure there are space and resources to support the variety and beauty of all bird species on earth.

Curlew (above)

BIRDS OF PREY

There are more than 500 birds of prey (also known as raptors) across the world, including eagles, owls, falcons, and hawks. They come in many different shapes and sizes, but they all have one thing in common—they eat flesh. Using their sharp talons and hooked beaks, they grab and kill their prey or feast on the bodies of animals that are already dead.

Meat eaters ➤ Perched patiently and hidden in the bushes, sparrowhawks can launch an attack at speeds of over 30 miles an hour. Their long legs give them a powerful push from their perch, and their short rounded wings and light body allow them to twist and turn easily. They fly very low to the ground, using their long tail to help them steer, and can tuck their wings in tightly to fit through the smallest of spaces. These clever birds have learned that garden birds resting on a feeder can offer an easy meal.

Fish eaters ➤ Seeing an osprey swoop down over the water and grasp a fish that sometimes weighs almost as much as it does is a magnificent sight. Pale-colored feathers on its belly help it to blend in with the bright sky, making it difficult for fish to spot. As it swoops down over the surface of the water, its wings

stretch out wide to slow its descent and its long legs extend to grab its prey. Rough scales on its feet hold the wriggling fish in place, and elongated, curved, and backward-facing talons spear the flesh to secure it while a long, hooked beak tears the flesh from the bones. Ospreys can even close their nostrils to keep out water during dives, and they have dense, oily plumage, which prevents their feathers from getting waterlogged.

Fish is a high-protein meal, and other raptors take advantage of this: fish eagles such as the American bald eagle (so-called because, from a distance, the white feathers on its head make it look bald) are also masters of the water, feasting on enormous Pacific salmon as well as waterbirds, such as egrets, which live close by. These eagles also build impressive nests, which the same pair adds to every year when they return to breed.

Sparrowhawk (above)

Osprey

Golden eagles ➤ A mythical-like creature, the golden eagle can spot a rodent from over a mile away and a rabbit from nearly double that distance. It's no wonder, then, that we use the phrase "eagle eye" to mean someone with very good eyesight! Soaring over remote mountains, this magnificent bird gets its name from the golden tinges on its head and neck feathers.

Golden eagle (left)

Extreme birds

Birds of prey are found across the globe, from the tiny pygmy falcon that lives in the African bush to the huge Andean condor that soars over some of the world's highest mountains.

Fastest The fastest animals on the planet, peregrine falcons, are able to hurtle through the air at over 200 miles an hour and strike their prey with military precision. To reach such an impressive speed, they pull in their wings and dive from a great height using gravity to increase their speed—a move known as a stoop. The streamlined body shape they create is so effective that designers have modeled fighter planes on it.

Largest and smallest The largest bird of prey in the world is the Andean condor, weighing in at up to 30 pounds and with a wingspan of nearly 10 feet. It soars over the Andes Mountains in South America to find food, using its broad wings to cover huge distances. Condors have keen eyesight, which helps them spot dead animals to feed on. In contrast, the black-thighed falconet is the smallest bird of prey in the world. It has a wingspan ten times smaller than the Andean condor and weighs just over an ounce. These tiny birds are agile enough to feed on butterflies and they have learned to select only the species that aren't poisonous to feed to their chicks.

Tallest The tallest bird of prey, and surely one of the most unusual, is the secretary bird. A resident of Africa, it has a distinctive crest and a very long tail and stands nearly four feet tall. It is capable of soaring flight but spends most of its time walking on its long legs. Most birds of prey grab their victim with sharp talons, but secretary birds do things differently—they kick their prey instead! Small insects only need to be stamped on a few times, but larger prey, such as snakes and hares, need a display of kickboxing behavior that is almost comical! However, they have a softer side too: males and females have impressive courtship displays and pair up for life, sleeping side by side in their nests.

Baldest There are around 15 species of vulture found in Europe, Asia, and Africa, and they mostly feed on carrion (the remains of prey killed by other predators). Many types of vultures have bald necks. This might not look very appealing, but it's thought that the lack of feathers is helpful when they thrust their necks deep inside carcasses to feed, as any feathers would get caked in blood. New research suggests that vultures have bald heads and necks to help them regulate their body temperature.

Secretary bird

Owls

We tend to think of owls as creatures of the night, but some species prefer to hunt during the day and others at dusk and dawn. You can tell when each species of owl prefers to hunt by looking at the color of its eyes.

Yellow eyes ✒ Owls that have yellow eyes have widespread hunting habits. The great gray owl can hunt at any time of day or night but prefers the early morning and late afternoon. They are an impressive sight to see as they soar over the snow-covered ground in search of small rodents, which they can hear moving beneath a blanket of up to a foot of snow.

Orange eyes ✒ Most owls that have orange eyes are crepuscular, which means that they are active around dawn and dusk. These owls, such as large Eurasian eagle-owls with their distinctive ear tufts, hunt prey including mice, rabbits, and birds. Eurasian eagle owls prefer remote places and, while they are mostly nocturnal, they can sometimes be seen hunting early and late in the day.

Dark eyes ✒ Brown or black eyes indicate an owl that hunts under the cover of darkness. You are more likely to hear these owls than see them. The barred owl of North America is famous for a distinctive series of hoots, which sounds like someone saying, "Who cooks for you? Who cooks for you all?" Owls that hunt at night fly completely silently, as the slightest sound could alert prey to their presence. A fine covering of down over their wing feathers helps the owls to surprise their prey by muffling the sound of air passing through their feathers.

Hearing ✒ Hearing is perhaps the sense that some owls, like the barn owl, rely on more than any other bird. Despite their big eyes, barn owls cannot see much better than we do in the dark, but their hearing is excellent, which helps them to catch fast-moving small mammals in complete darkness without using their eyesight at all. Their ears are unusual – the left ear opening is slightly higher than the right one, which means that sounds from below reach the right ear before the left one, helping the owl to pinpoint exactly where the sounds are coming from. Along with this, a barn owl's face is surrounded by stiff feathers, which create a heart-shaped ruff. This channels sounds toward the owl's ears, a bit like a satellite dish, helping to magnify the sound.

Long-eared owl (left)

SEABIRDS

The sea is a challenging place to live, but many birds are highly adapted to life on the open ocean and only come ashore to mate and breed. Seabirds are found from the shoreline to the open ocean and feed in many different ways: gannets and terns dive into the water from great heights to catch their target, cormorants chase fish underwater, and gulls pick their prey off the water's surface.

Waders ➤ Oystercatchers, sandpipers, avocets, and phalaropes are often found along the shoreline where water meets the land. In areas where they migrate, these birds will flock together to provide safety in numbers. Different species feed on the variety of high-protein invertebrates that lie hidden in the mud. Many waders have sensitive nerve endings at the end of their beaks, which enable them to feel prey hidden in mud or soft soil. Some larger species, particularly those adapted to drier habitats, will eat larger prey, including insects and small reptiles.

Often the length of a bird's beak can give you a clue to what they eat. The extremely elegant, long beak of the curlew, with its curved end, allows these birds to grab food hiding deep in the mud that birds with shorter beaks, such as dunlin and turnstone, just can't reach. Redshanks, with their bright orange-red legs, have long beaks too, allowing them to search deep into the mud for worms and crustaceans.

Curlews (above)

Redshank (above) Oystercatcher (below)

Seabirds of warmer waters

Seabirds are found in every ocean across the globe—warmer waters offer bountiful food and many tropical seabirds are more colorful than their colder water cousins.

Blue-footed boobies ⌇ Blue is not a common color for a bird's beak and feet, but it certainly stands out on the blue-footed boobies found in the Galapagos. The bluer their feet, the more attractive a male is to a potential mate. Males perform strange dance moves, showing off their feet to curious females with a high-stepping strut.

Frigatebirds ⌇ Male frigatebirds are distinctive with their dark plumage, long forked tails, and enormous red throat sacs, which they inflate to attract a mate. Strangely for a seabird, they are not good swimmers and don't even have waterproof feathers! However, they are experts at stealing food from other birds or snatching it from the water's surface.

Terns ⌇ Terns are slender seabirds and can be found worldwide. When it comes to breeding, they have little or no regard for nest building and many make their nests in little more than a bare scrape in the ground! The white tern takes this to the extreme, laying an egg directly onto a branch with no protection from the elements. Although the branch offers protection from ground predators, there is still a huge risk that high winds will knock the egg off its perch. However, should disaster strike, the mother tern is quick to lay a new egg and take the risk all over again.

Blue-footed boobies

Seabirds of colder waters

Since they spend most of their lives out at sea, we learn most about seabirds from studying them during their brief time on land, mostly when they're nesting and breeding on isolated islands away from predators and human threats. A visit to a seabird colony is an amazing experience—the sight and sound, not to mention the smell, is unforgettable!

Gulls ➴ Gulls are an incredibly successful group of birds. Intelligent and resourceful, many have moved from their coastal habitats into towns and cities to take advantage of the leftovers and habitats created by humans. They have gained a reputation for stealing food and attacking and mobbing other birds.

Great black-backed gulls ➴ Aggressive predators that patrol colonies of nesting puffins,

these birds are always on the hunt for sick and injured adults and unattended chicks who might stray from the safety of their underground burrows.

Kittiwakes ➴ In contrast, kittiwakes, with their black-tipped wings, are smaller. Their name is derived from their shrill "kittee-wa-aaake" call.

Great black-backed gull and puffins (above)

Gannets ➤ One of the world's most impressive seabirds is the gannet. They nest in colonies like vast cities, which are busy, noisy, and smelly! Famous for their fish-eating ability, gannets hunt by diving into the sea at speeds of 60 miles an hour from an impressive height of up to 100 feet. This potentially fatal maneuver is made possible by a number of adaptations, including: nostrils hidden inside their mouth; air sacs in the face and chest, which cushion the impact when they dive into the water, and eyes located far forward on the face, allowing them to judge distances accurately.

Gannets (left)

FRESHWATER BIRDS

Living on water provides birds with food, a safe place away from many predators, and access to a bath! But it also means that they must remain waterproof and find a way to keep their young dry.

Waterfowl ⤳ When you visit a lake or river, waterfowl are the birds you will most likely see. Their webbed feet mean they are excellent swimmers. However, because their feet are placed so far back on their body (to push them along when swimming), it gives them a rather comical appearance as they waddle awkwardly on land!

Ducks ⤳ Ducks come in all shapes and sizes and live on salt water as well as fresh water. The common mallard is a firm favorite on waterways, often seen with its head down and tail feathers waggling up in the air, dabbling along the banks in search of food. The male mallards, or drakes, have very colorful feathers, but they molt in summer into what is known as their "eclipse" plumage. This makes them look more like the females, with their brown feathers.

Swans ⤳ Swans are elegant birds and are often a symbol of love because they stay with their partner for life. Not all swans are white—in Australia the only native swan is black. Bewick's swans have individual black and yellow markings on their beaks, which allow scientists to recognize different individuals and follow their progress from one year to the next, building up a unique story of each bird's life. This provides important information about their migration and breeding success. They breed in the cold Arctic tundra of Northern Russia; then some populations head west to spend the winter in northern Europe, others turn east toward China and Japan.

Grebes ⤳ The most striking thing about grebes is their courtship. The western grebes of North America participate in "rushing," where they sprint long distances over water. Using a combination of speedy footwork, forceful slaps on the water's surface with played feet, and an usual stride; these grebes seem to defy gravity in order to impress their mates! This is followed by an elaborate dance with their partners, holding a piece of weed in their beaks.

After hatching, the young chicks hitch a ride on their parent's back, hiding in the safety of their feathers.

Mallard, male (above)

Canada geese ✒ Canada geese are
famed for their V-shaped flying pattern,
called a skein. This distinctive formation helps
the birds to save energy by using the upward-
moving air (called lift) created by the bird flying in
front. The birds play fair, taking turns flying at the
front, as this position requires the most energy.

Canada geese

Flamingos 🦢 With their distinctive pink plumage, flamingos are water birds that tend to live on salty or very alkaline lakes or lagoons. The six species of flamingo have evolved to live in the harshest of environments due to some very unusual adaptations.

Their beak is uniquely designed to be used upside down and helps them to filter out tiny brine shrimps and blue-green algae from the water, which, when digested, give them their pink color.

The nest is a turret of mud, which raises the egg and chick up out of the rising water and keeps it dry. These turrets are a real feat of engineering, as their height and shape mean they act like a cooling tower: as air passes over the top of the nest, it is cooled to a few degrees less than the baking earth the nest is built on. Water is sucked up by the mud, evaporating at the top, which adds to the cooling effect for the young chicks. This provides the perfect environment for incubation.

Lesser flamingos have incredibly long legs—almost half their height! Being this tall means they are able to wade deeper in search of the organisms they feed on. Their legs are bare because delicate feathers would easily be damaged by the hot and salty water they spend much of their lives standing in.

Lesser flamingos (left)

Fish eaters

Fish may be the dish of choice for many birds, but catching them isn't necessarily very easy! Because of this, fish-eating birds have many clever and unusual ways to catch their slippery prey.

Pelicans ➤ These birds are skilled fishers, sometimes working as a team to herd fish into shallow water where they are easier to catch. They lunge forward to catch them in the huge leathery pouches that dangle below their beaks, using the upper bill as a lid. Hungry chicks wait impatiently in the nest, calling loudly for their dinner. They stick their beaks down the parents' throats, causing them to bring back up the half-digested fish.

Kingfishers ➤ These birds are patient hunters, sitting quietly on a perch and watching carefully until a flash of color grabs their attention, when they swiftly swoop down to seize their prey in their beak. Adults teach their young to hunt by dropping dead fish into the water for them to catch. After mastering this skill, they are chased away by the adult to find their own territory.

Herons ➤ One of the most impressive ways of feeding on fish is that adopted by the African black heron. It uses its wings to make a parasol, creating shade over the water—a trick known as canopy feeding. This reduces the glare and reflection on the surface of the water, making fish and shrimps easier to see. The shade may also actually encourage them to the surface, as shelter and shade can be attractive when you live in shallow open water. The heron relies on this fatal attraction in order to catch its prey.

Other species of heron rely on extreme patience and remaining still for long periods of time, ready for the perfect moment to dart toward their prey and snap it up from the water below. The green heron takes this to the extreme by using different objects such as sticks, feathers, and even discarded popcorn as lures to attract the fish. This is a rare example of tool-use in birds.

Kingfisher (above)

Black herons

FLIGHTLESS BIRDS

Flightless birds have wings and feathers, but unlike other birds, they cannot soar through the sky. More than 50 bird species across the world stay firmly on the ground (or on water), and there are many others who choose not to fly very often.

True flightless birds

Kiwis ➤ In New Zealand, the national bird is the kiwi. This nocturnal creature, with nostrils at the end of its beak, snuffles around in the undergrowth looking for worms. Its tiny wings are covered in long, thin feathers, which look more like fluffy little hairs. Sadly, rats and possums are a huge threat to these appealing, ground-nesting birds, as they steal eggs and kill defenseless chicks.

Kākāpōs ➤ Sometimes known as the "owl parrot" because of the circular discs around its eyes, the kākāpō is the only flightless parrot and the heaviest one in the world. These nocturnal foragers have strong legs and move around the ground in a clumsy, hopping jog. They are also great climbers and can scale tall trees, using their wings to help "parachute" back down to the forest floor. Numbers of these flightless parrots were once dangerously low, but thanks to a successful breeding program using the latest technology, and with a long life expectancy (over 90 years), the species seems to be on the road to recovery.

Ostrich, male (above)

Southern cassowaries The southern cassowary is an impressive and brightly-colored bird related to the kiwi and ostrich. It is one of the few birds that is known to have attacked and even killed a human. Tall and fast, these birds feed mainly on fruits, shoots, and occasionally small animals. They are normally shy, but when provoked, they defend themselves. At the top of their bright blue head is a thick casque (a sort of helmet), which grows into a large dome as the birds get older. Scientists have argued about its use, but one theory is that it is used to headbutt their enemies. However, these birds' true weapons are on their feet: each of their three toes bears a deadly claw, the longest of which can measure up to four inches and can slice through flesh. Attacking cassowaries charge and kick, leaping high into the air and sometimes jumping on top of their victim. Thankfully, attacks are rare in their native Australia, but they are still powerful and cheeky enough to break into people's homes!

Ostriches The heaviest and largest flightless bird is the ostrich. Reaching over eight feet tall, ostriches are true record-breakers. They have the largest eyes of any bird—which are three times bigger than a human eye! They also have an unusual way of looking after their eggs and keeping them warm. More than 50 eggs can be found in one nest, all laid by a number of different females. The dominant female will tend to the nest during the day with the dominant male taking over at night. This female's eggs will always be at the center of the group, staying warmer and more protected than those around them, which gives them a greater chance of hatching.

Ostrich, female

Penguins

Penguins are the largest group of flightless birds. They are often associated with the chilly waters of the Antarctic but, out of the 18 species, many are found elsewhere. They may not be able to fly in the air, but they are the masters of soaring underwater. Agile and speedy swimmers, they have much shorter wings than birds that fly through the sky, which helps to propel them forward through water, which is much denser than air. The legs are set far back on their body and, together with the help of their tail, they form an underwater rudder that enables them to hunt down to great depths of close to 2000 feet. These incredible birds can hold their breath for around 20 minutes at a time.

Little penguins ➤ The smallest species of penguin is the little penguin (also known as the fairy or blue penguin), which lives in the waters off New Zealand and southern Australia. The distinctive blue color of the adults is clearly visible on their head, back, wings, and tail. A quarter of the height and a fraction of the weight of their giant emperor cousins, they are secretive birds, only coming ashore at night. They nest and hide in burrows or inside small crevices among the rocks close to the water's edge. What these tiny birds lack in size, they make up for in volume—they are very noisy! This might be a defense mechanism to frighten off any predators without revealing their tiny size.

Gentoo penguins ➤ This species can move through water faster than any other bird, and they can also leap out of the water rather than swimming through it! This method of swimming is similar to the way dolphins swim and is called porpoising. This is less energy efficient than staying completely submerged, but it allows the birds to breathe more regularly, meaning they can swim much longer distances at greater speeds. Scientists also think that they may do this to confuse both marine predators and prey, which may not be expecting swimming birds to leave and reenter the water. Whatever the reason, it looks like they are having fun!

African penguins ⇘ Native to southern Africa, these noisy birds are also called jackass penguins because of their call, which sounds like a braying donkey.

One of four species of "banded" penguin, they have a band of black that runs across their chests, black beaks with a small vertical white band, and spotted bellies with patterns as unique as our fingerprints. They are one of the few species of penguin that have to worry about temperatures getting too high rather than too low. In their habitat, there is a risk of sunstroke and their eggs cooking in the midday sun, which can be more dangerous than the sub-zero conditions that some of their relatives have to cope with.

When temperatures get too hot for these birds, their blood is diverted to a pink gland just above their eyes, which is unfeathered. This allows it to be cooled by the air surrounding it, causing the gland to turn a darker shade of pink.

Emperor penguins ⇘ Perhaps the most famous of all the species of penguin is the emperor penguin. It is also the largest and lives in huge groups of thousands of birds. Finding your chick among so many isn't easy, but incredibly, when parents return from their hunting expeditions, they recognize the calls of their own chicks and are able to find them in the huge colony of identical-looking birds.

Emperor penguins

Occasional fliers

Some birds that are able to fly do so only occasionally and usually as a means to escape from predators. Others use their wings to propel themselves forward, but not necessarily in full flight.

Great bustards ➤ Great bustards hold the record for being the heaviest living flying animal, which might explain why they would rather run than fly if threatened. Males are much larger than females, with a body weight of around 40 pounds, and so find it very hard to get airborne. But what these birds lack in flying ability, they make up for in courtship behavior—there are often violent clashes between males, who ram into each other with their beaks. Their displays to potential mates are also flamboyant—the males strut around and puff up their throats to the size of a football.

Chickens ➤ Domestic chickens have lost the ability to fly, due to selective breeding by humans to increase the size of the bird's breast meat. Chickens are the most numerous birds, with over 19 billion of them living around the world. Their wild ancestors, the red junglefowl, can fly almost vertically but only for rapid bursts in order to escape predators. Other game birds, such as pheasants, can do the same, and the fact that they can't fly very well means that they have become a popular game bird for shooting.

Tinamous ➤ Flight involves a complicated series of maneuvers. Most birds make it look easy, but winning the prize for the most uncoordinated flight are the tinamous. They spend much of their lives on the ground and only become airborne when they need to escape from ground predators. They are heavy birds, and when they attempt to take off, fly, and land with their inadequately short wings and tails, they frequently lose control, even colliding with trees and rocks. These birds are not very well designed for life in the air—they have a small heart, blood vessels, and lungs in comparison to other birds of their size. When they do finally get airborne, it's not for very long, as they can only usually travel for very short distances.

Domestic chickens (left)

TROPICAL BIRDS

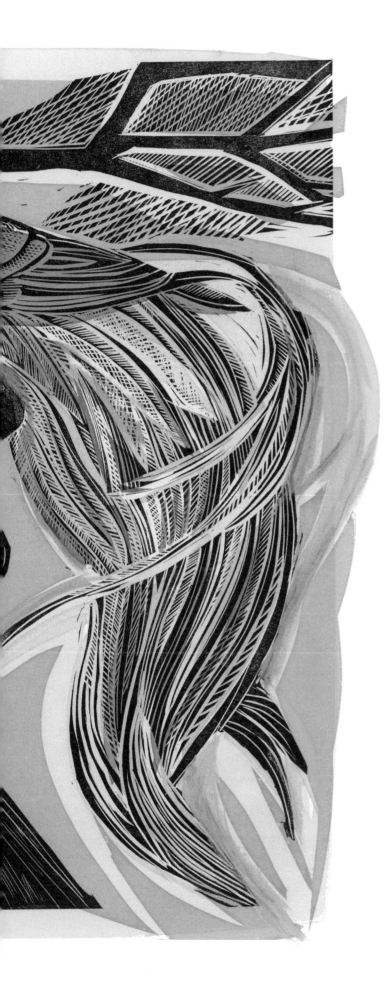

In the tropics, many birds are bright, colorful, and have loud and sometimes unusual calls. Rainforests are packed with a range of incredible species with dazzling plumage and bizarre courtship displays, visible from the canopy to the forest floor.

Stunning plumage ➤ The scarlet macaw is one of the world's most colorful birds, with feathers of red, orange, yellow, and blue. These large parrots have an unusual way of dealing with toxins in their food—they eat large amounts of clay, which seems to neutralize the effect of anything poisonous. They also have extremely adaptable beaks, tongues, and feet, which they use to crack open nutshells and pick out the seeds inside. They are regarded as one of the most intelligent species of bird and are able to "speak," copying many human words. However, because of this, they are often kept as pets, and many live their lives confined to cages rather than soaring free over the rainforest canopy.

Male Raggiana birds of paradise, found in Papua New Guinea, are real show-offs! They have extremely long, bright orange feathers, which form a sort of "tail" but actually originate from underneath the wing. Their courtship display is spectacular, with feather shaking, wing clapping, and head shaking.

The national bird of Peru, the Andean cock-of-the-rock stands out among the cloud forests with its intensely-colored orange plumage, crested head, and elaborate courtship dance. Males gather in a small group called a lek, while the females watch them. The males flap their wings, bob and bow their heads, clap their beaks, and make crowing sounds—all of which the females find very attractive!

Perilous plumage ➤ Many tropical birds have elaborate and extravagant plumage. However, these beautiful feathers are sometimes the reason why these tropical birds are hunted. Some communities wear the brightly colored feathers in ceremonial dress, and collectors and traders hunt these bright creatures as prized trophies. Those that look the most stunning have suffered the worst, and many species of birds of paradise are endangered as a result.

Raggiana birds of paradise, male (left)

Bowerbirds

Bowerbirds Bowerbirds are fascinating to watch, with their elaborate architectural skills. Male satin bowerbirds gain their deep blue-black feathers when they reach around seven years old. After this, a great deal of time and effort is spent on attracting a female to mate. The male spends many hours building a bower—a U-shaped structure with parallel walls of twigs—and then goes about collecting colored objects to decorate it with.

Satin bowerbirds love the color blue, which accentuates the males' blue feathers. In order to impress a female, a male will travel far and wide to find blue objects—some are natural, like feathers and flowers, but often he will include human-made items like plastic straws, bottle tops, pegs, and even toothbrushes! His decorating skills don't end at merely collecting objects—he may also "paint" the inside of his bower with a mixture of plant material and saliva.

The male is extremely fussy about his artistic handiwork and will carefully rearrange items if they fall out of place. Competition for the best decorations is fierce: males have even been known to steal blue objects from others close by! Once everything is in order, he will start to dance, tempting the female inside his bower to mate with her. The dance consists of a flamboyant display of exaggerated movements: strutting and bowing, stretching and quivering wings. He also calls and buzzes to impress her. The final touch is giving one of the precious blue items to her.

But the females are very choosy and will visit several different bowers before deciding on which mate they prefer. For some males, all this effort is wasted—even after days of work on their bower, their attempts to win over a female will be unsuccessful.

Satin bowerbirds, male (left), female (right)

Extremes

Smallest bird ✒ The smallest birds
on the planet are the hummingbirds. Tiny
iridescent jewels in flight, they live life in the
fast lane, beating their wings up to 80 times a
second, creating an audible hum. Holding the
record is the bee hummingbird, which weighs
less than two paper clips. These tiny birds
also have the smallest eggs—three thousand
eggs would make up the weight of one
ostrich egg. They feed mainly on energy-
rich nectar, which is in plentiful supply from
the many tropical flowers.

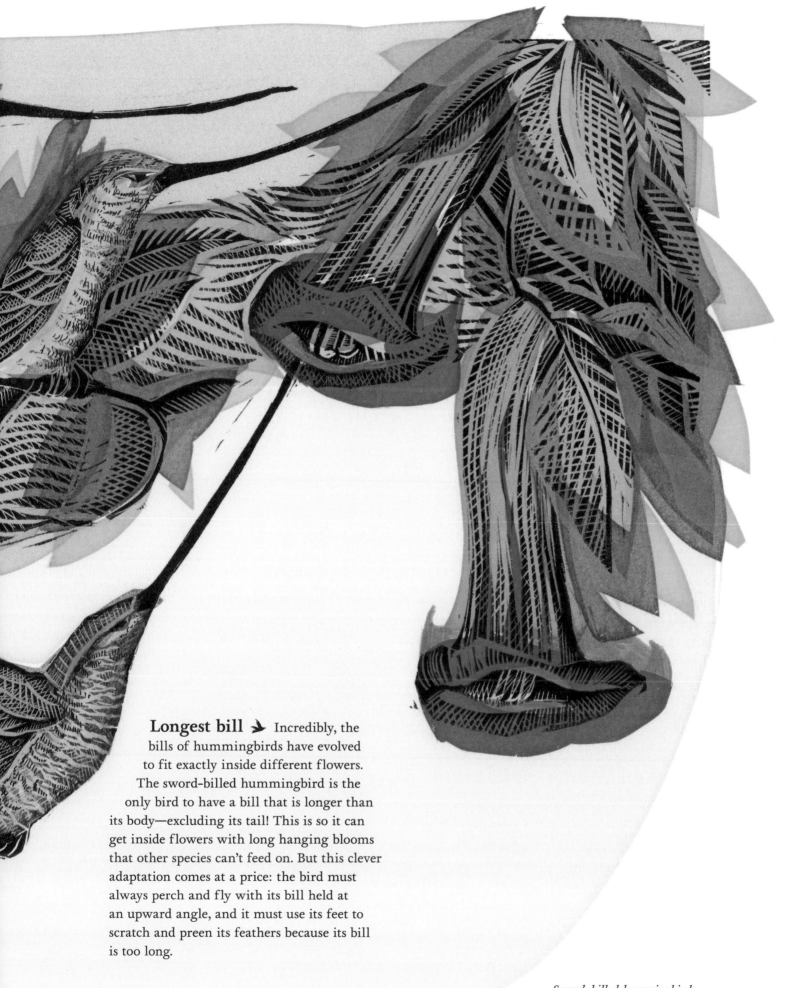

Longest bill ✦ Incredibly, the
bills of hummingbirds have evolved
to fit exactly inside different flowers.
The sword-billed hummingbird is the
only bird to have a bill that is longer than
its body—excluding its tail! This is so it can
get inside flowers with long hanging blooms
that other species can't feed on. But this clever
adaptation comes at a price: the bird must
always perch and fly with its bill held at
an upward angle, and it must use its feet to
scratch and preen its feathers because its bill
is too long.

Sword-billed hummingbirds

Smelliest ➤ In the tropics, you don't have to look beautiful to stand out from the crowd—the stink bird or hoatzin does this by using its scent! It is one of the few birds in the world to have a diet consisting mostly of leaves. As they are digested, the leaves ferment in the bird's gut, giving off the smell of fresh cow manure! Digestion happens very slowly and can often take nearly two full days, which explains its rather slow pace of life. These birds spend their time perched on branches over tropical waterways. They can't swim or fly very far and often topple off and fall into the water! For a young chick, this could be fatal, but these peculiar birds have another trick up their sleeve—the chicks have claws at the ends of their wings, which help them climb around until their feathers grow.

Poisonous ➤ The hooded pitohui, found in New Guinea, is considered to be unique among bird species. This is because this amazing bird possesses the same neurotoxin in its feathers that is found in the skins of poisonous frogs in South America! There is not enough poison to kill a human, but, after taking one bite, a predator is sure to give this bird a wide berth.

Tools ➤ Only a small number of animals have been known to use tools. The palm cockatoo is one such bird that is able to create a musical instrument and make a sound with it! Males use this extraordinary talent to impress females. They begin by selecting a dead, hollow eucalyptus tree as a sounding board and use their feet or a nut to bang on it to make themselves known to members of the opposite sex. Some males are even able to select sticks, clean off the leaves and bark, and trim them to around 7 or 8 inches long to make a drumstick! Holding this with their foot, they then beat rhythmically on the hollow tree. The sound fills the area and hopefully attracts a female. Such a complex use of tools indicates their remarkable intelligence.

Palm cockatoo (left)

TREE DWELLERS

Forests and woodlands are home to a huge variety of birds. Many birds choose to perch or make their home in the treetops, as the height offers them a vantage point to search for food and it is also a safer place to nest than on the ground, where there is a greater risk of predators.

Trees for drumming ➤ Woodpeckers are famous for their drumming behavior, communicating over long distances by hammering their beaks against hollow branches and trunks. These noisy birds select hollow branches and trees that make the loudest and clearest sound. You'd expect that all the banging would give them a headache, but they have specially thick skulls to protect their brains from damage.

Acorn woodpeckers ➤ Acorn woodpeckers, which are found in western American woodlands, use their sharp beaks to clear out old tree cavities where they set up home. Often several females will come together to lay their eggs in a single hole, and the birds will work together in family groups to raise their young and gather, store, and guard food. The trees they build their nests in also supply a plentiful source of food in the form of insects and tree sap, but most importantly acorns, which the birds are famous for hoarding in trees called granaries. They drill individual holes in the granaries and then gather huge collections of acorns there. One granary tree may have up to 50,000 holes in it!

When a woodpecker abandons its nest cavity, it is sometimes reused. The great hornbill of southeast Asia is one species that does this. After finding a suitable tree hole, the female will line it with nest material. When she is ready to lay her egg, she and her mate will seal up the entrance with droppings, leaving a gap barely wide enough for the tip of her bill to poke through. Inside this secure nest, she molts her feathers and, to keep things clean, she even projects her droppings out of the tiny hole—a trick the chick learns as well! But the only way she can get food is through this tiny crack, so she is reliant on her mate to find the next meal and to feed her through the small opening. When the chick hatches, it spends about two months inside the chamber with its mother before they both break out. Although this may sound a bit like a prison, this strategy is very successful at protecting the young chicks from predators, such as tree snakes.

Acorn woodpeckers

Trees for camouflage

Trees offer excellent protection and camouflage to hide nocturnal birds during the day. Many birds sport dull brown or mottled feathers, which blend in with the bark on the trunk.

Tawny frogmouths ➤ The nocturnal Australian tawny frogmouth is the master of disguise. Often confused with an owl, it is perfectly camouflaged against the tree bark where it rests during the day. This clever bird will even close its eyes and mouth and hold up its head and beak at such an angle that it looks just like a broken tree limb to complete the illusion! If there is a threat nearby, parents will call out in alarm, signaling to their chicks to remain still and retain their camouflage. If the threat gets too close, they will flash their bright yellow eyes and huge yellow mouth to startle the predator, just long enough to make their escape.

Potoos ➤ Nicknamed 'poor-me-ones' because of their very sad and haunting call, potoos are found in Central and South America. These nocturnal hunters look slightly out of proportion, with very large heads in comparison to their body size and with similarly large eyes to help them forage at night. However, these big yellow eyes could give them away to potential predators during the day so they have to keep them closed—something that might make them vulnerable to predators. But potoos have an unusual way of keeping an eye on things: their eyelids have slits that enable them to detect movement and therefore possible threats, even when their eyes are closed! Their camouflaged plumage means they blend in perfectly with the trees they spend their days perched on. These stumps also provide a place to lay their single, spotted egg, without the need to build a nest.

Tawny frogmouths

Trees for food

Trees offer a huge variety of food for birds from insects, fruits, and seeds to something a bit sweeter. Many birds spend their time foraging in among the leaves, branches, and bark, safe from ground-dwelling predators.

Nuthatches ➤ Upside-down foragers, nuthatches feast on insects hidden in or under the bark. Their diet is varied, including nuts and seeds, and their name comes from a habit of wedging nuts and other bits of food into a crevice and then hacking at them with their strong bills. These birds plan ahead, storing seeds in tree crevices or hidden in the ground to use when food is scarce.

Greater honeyguides ➤ It's not just birds who nest in trees; a variety of other creatures choose to live here, too. Bees nest high up and away from ground predators, and some birds have developed a taste for them and their honey. A gray-brown relative of the woodpecker, the greater honeyguide loves to feast on bee grubs and can even digest beeswax. These bee-loving birds have a remarkable relationship with local tribes and have even been known to guide humans to the location of a hive. In East Africa, the Borana Oromo people have learned to work with honeyguides to track down hives. The bird indicates when it

has found a hive by stopping and calling. The hunters then calm the bees by using smoke while the nest is opened and the honey is taken. The bird feeds on what is left in the hive and the tribe often leaves it a present of honey as a thank-you.

Yellow-bellied sapsuckers ➤ The yellow-bellied sapsucker is a type of North American woodpecker. Its name is misleading, as they don't actually suck the sap out of the tree. Instead they lick the sap up using their long tongues, which have stiff hairs on the tip. They harvest sap from birch and maple trees by producing a neat line of holes in the tree bark, causing the sap to flow out. Scientists think that there may even be something in their saliva that causes the sap to run more freely! But their diets aren't restricted to just sweet sugary sap; the birds also feast on insects that are attracted to the sticky liquid. However, these birds are often considered to be pests, as many of the trees they feed upon end up dying due to the damage inflicted by these birds.

Common blackbirds, male (above)

Yellow-bellied sapsuckers

PASSERINES

Passerines, also known as perching birds, are by far the largest group of birds, with over half of all known species falling into this category. With over 5,000 species, this group is incredibly diverse. However, one thing is common to them—their four long flexible toes, three that point forward and one that points backward. When the chicks hatch, they are naked, blind, and helpless. They need to be fed and cared for, which requires a great deal of effort from the parents.

Intelligence ➤ The largest passerine is the common raven, which belongs to a group called the corvids. This group includes crows, rooks, and magpies, species that are often considered to be among the most intelligent of birds. These birds have a remarkable ability to solve problems in order to find food, in some cases performing better than young children or chimpanzees! They have been known to pick up sticks in order to get grubs out of holes in trees, and studies have shown that ravens will try to deceive each other by pretending to put food in one place while really hiding it in another spot. Crows have also been observed dropping hard nuts onto roads and waiting for cars to drive over them, then hopping back onto the road to retrieve the contents—an easy and innovative way of cracking them open!

Cooperative breeders ➤ A small number of bird species rely on extra family members (normally juveniles or other adults) to help raise their young. The Australian superb fairy wren is just one example of a species that breeds communally. Juveniles from an earlier brood often remain with their parents for a year or more to help raise the next brood, helping to tidy the nest and protect it from brood parasites, such as cuckoos. This takes the strain off the parents and results in a larger proportion of the brood surviving and leaving the nest.

Eurasian magpies (above)

Superb fairy wrens, male (left) female (right)

The most numerous ➴ Red-billed queleas, found in sub-Saharan Africa, are renowned for being the most numerous birds in the world. They feed on cereal crops, so they have been labeled pests and their numbers are often controlled in extreme ways, including chemicals being sprayed on roosting sites. However, this has little effect, as their populations migrate over large distances to find new food sources. As a flock flies overhead, the sky darkens with the number of birds. It resembles a rolling cloud.

Brood parasites ➴ Cuckoos are well known for laying their eggs in other birds' nests but they are not alone in this sneaky behavior. Brown-headed cowbirds invest their time and energy into laying as many eggs as they can in the nests of over 200 other species. Females are capable of laying as many as 40 eggs in one season. In most cases, these eggs will hatch and be raised by the host species as their own. The chicks either push the other eggs out of the nest or compete with the other chicks, causing them to starve to death.

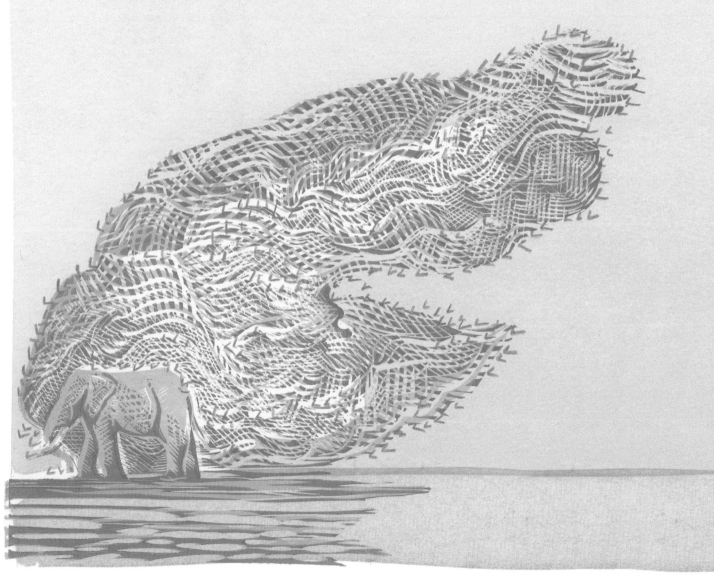

Red-billed queleas

Blood feeders ❧ Bird species have varied diets, feeding on everything from berries and seeds to insects and shellfish—some even feed on mammal blood. The red-billed oxpecker can be spotted hitching a ride on the backs of giraffes, rhinoceroses, and buffaloes. They feed on blood-filled ticks attached to these African giants and rid the host of any irritation. However, the relationship often takes a more sinister turn when the oxpecker pecks at the mammal's wounds to keep them open so it has a constant supply of blood.

This unusual taste for blood isn't unique. Vampire finches also feed on blood. However, unlike red-billed oxpeckers, they mainly feed on the blood of other birds. Blue-footed boobies are often the preferred choice and they seem to put up little resistance—perhaps because they think they are being rid of parasites by the finches!

Red-billed oxpeckers

Garden birds

Passerines include many common garden birds. Titmice, finches, blackbirds, and robins are among a group called the songbirds.

Blue tits Blue tits are cheery birds and can be spotted fluttering around seed feeders in a flurry of blue, yellow, white, and green. They are, in fact, woodland birds but have found European gardens and parks ideal places to live in. Devoted parents, they can lay clutches of between 7 and 13 eggs. They invest a huge amount of energy in their offspring, and the male and female take turns visiting their youngsters, each time with a tasty caterpillar.

Robins One of everyone's favorite garden birds is the robin—it is bold and has a habit of following gardeners around, hoping for easy pickings in the newly dug ground. Worms and insects are their favorite food, and they have even been known to take food from a human hand. But this cute and fluffy exterior hides a slightly darker side, as robins are also very aggressive defenders of their territories and will fight rivals to the death.

Robin

Finches ➤ Bullfinches, chaffinches, and goldfinches each have differently-shaped beaks, which have evolved over time to suit their specific diets. The bullfinch has a short, stubby beak, specially adapted for feeding on buds. The chaffinch has a short, thick, and cone-shaped beak, which it uses to prise seeds from hard shells. The goldfinch has a long, fine beak, which allows it to extract seeds from thistles and teasels.

Also a member of the finch family, the distinctive crossbill takes beak evolution to the extreme. Found in boreal forests (which contain many evergreen trees), the tips of this bird's beak do not meet at a point but instead cross over. It uses this clever tool to extract seeds from ripe pine cones.

Bullfinch, male (above)

FEATHERS

Birds are covered in feathers—a typical songbird has a few thousand, while a swan can have up to 25,000. Different types of feathers have different purposes. Protecting birds from the cold are the fluffy down feathers, which lie closest to the body. On top of these lie a layer of contour feathers, which are short and round and help make the bird streamlined during flight. Then there are different types of flight feathers: primary flight feathers, which can be found at the end of the wing and provide power and maneuverability, and secondary flight feathers, which help shape the wing in a curve and provide lift-off. The tail feathers are used for steering, balance, and braking.

Barn owl (above)

Being lightweight is critical for birds, so their feathers (and skeleton) are designed to be strong but light enough to make their flight as efficient as possible. Feathers are made from keratin, which is the same material that our hair and fingernails are made from. Keratin is resilient to wear and tear and is the ideal material to cope with the stresses and strains of flying, particularly during long migrations.

Feathers need frequent attention to keep them working properly. Most birds spend several hours a day bathing and arranging their feathers to keep them clean. They also cover their feathers in a special waterproof oil from a gland just under the tail, called the preen gland.

Birds use their wings in different ways. Sandgrouse live in the desert where water is scarce. To ensure their chicks don't dehydrate, male birds seek out a waterhole and dip their feathers into the water. Their feathers are specially adapted to soak up water, like a sponge, which they can then carry back to their nests.

Owls ➤ These birds are silent fliers due to clever adaptations of their feathers. Those on the front edge of their wings are covered in small structures that help to break up the airflow. The trailing edge of their wings has a fringe, which breaks up the airflow even further. Together, these adaptations result in a huge reduction in the noise of the air passing over the wings. This, combined with very downy feathers on their wings and legs which further absorb noise, results in a silent wing beat—essential for swooping down on prey at night.

Short-eared owl

BEAKS AND EYES

Beaks are used in many different ways—for eating, cleaning, killing prey, fighting, searching for food, courtship, feeding young, and much more. They come in many shapes and sizes, and each one has evolved for a different use. The long, sharp beak of the heron is like a dagger, used for spearing fish before tossing them into the air and swallowing them, while parrots use their strong sharp beaks for cracking open hard-shelled nuts. Flamingos have bills that have adapted to work like a sieve as they feed on tiny algae in the water. Warblers use their slender beaks to fit into narrow crevices and pick up small, wriggling bugs from amongst bark and leaves.

Willow warblers (above)

The egg tooth ✏ Breaking out of a hard-shelled egg is quite a feat for a tiny chick. That's why chicks have a sharp protrusion at the tip of their beak, the egg tooth, which helps them to crack and break out of their shell. Without this, they would be trapped!

Eyes ✏ Relative to their size, birds have very large eyes. Good eyesight is essential for flying safely, catching prey, and foraging. Birds' eyes are fixed in their heads, meaning that they can't move them in the same way we can. Instead, they have to turn their whole head in the direction of the object in order to see it. The position of the eye indicates whether they are predators or prey.

Owls (predators) have front-facing eyes like humans, which means they lack the peripheral vision that some birds have. However, they have

an incredible perception of depth and distance, which they use to catch their prey. Their eyes have a very large retina, giving them fantastic vision in low light, but they can only see in black and white.

Robins (prey) have eyes that sit on the sides of their head, giving them nearly all-round peripheral vision, essential to spot potential predators. In order to look down for food, they must tilt their heads so one eye looks down and the other looks up. This way they can keep one eye on their food and the other on the sky and any potential danger.

Waders (prey), who spend much of their time looking for food with their bills in mud or sand, have eyes near the back of their head. This gives them a good view of what's behind them when their heads are down and they are feeding.

Redshanks

NESTS

Birds use their nests as a place to lay eggs and raise their chicks. They are found in all different shapes and sizes, from a small hole in the ground to elaborate structures that can be made out of a range of surprising materials, such as rocks and spit!

Burrows ➤ Seabirds, like puffins, have learned to use their surroundings to make their nests. They sometimes use abandoned rabbit burrows and can also dig their own burrows on the remote islands where they breed. In the spring, they excavate these burrows, returning to the same one year after year to lay their single egg. Hidden deep underground, the growing chick is protected from hungry gulls, which patrol the area in search of an easy meal.

Rocks ➤ The rock wren does not opt for soft surroundings for its nest. Instead, it chooses rocky crevices and lines these with grass, animal hair, and feathers. The finishing touch is a selection of stones, which form a pathway up to its nest.

Weaving ➤ Many types of bird choose to weave vegetation to construct nests. Blackbirds and robins build nests in what most of us consider to be a "classic" bird's nest design—a cup shape, composed of grasses and small twigs woven together, camouflaged with moss and lined with grass. The masters of weaving, though, have to be the weaver birds. They create very elaborate masterpieces that often take many years to perfect. Grass and leaves are interwoven over several days to form a hanging structure with an entrance and an egg chamber. This process is taken to a whole new level by sociable weavers who put in a collective effort, creating a structure that more than 500 birds can live in at any one time.

Weaver birds (above)

Saliva ➤ The cave-dwelling edible-nest swiftlet makes its nest out of spit produced by well-developed salivary glands in its mouth, which get bigger during the breeding season. The strands of saliva become hard when exposed to the air and form a glue that holds the nest together and attaches it to the cave wall.

Eggs ➤ Eggs vary in size and shape depending on where a bird lives and the amount of calcium in its diet. Some are round at both ends, while others have a more distinctive "egg" shape. There are numerous explanations for this but it certainly gives them strength to withstand the weight of the parent bird during incubation, and recently it has been discovered that the flying ability of the species dictates the shape—faster and longer fliers tend to have pointier eggs!

Color ➤ It's not just the size of the egg that varies from species to species; the color of birds' eggs differs too. Birds that lay their eggs in holes or anywhere dark, such as kingfishers, are likely to have eggs that are either white or pale blue, as this helps the birds locate their eggs in the dark.

Birds that lay their eggs in the open or on the ground need them to be well camouflaged, and these eggs tend to be speckled with spots or patterns. Brown and mottled, lapwing eggs are barely visible among their surroundings of stones, which makes them virtually invisible to hungry predators.

Cuckoos ➤ Cuckoos are famous for laying their eggs in the nests of other birds. Amazingly, cuckoo eggs are different colors depending on which bird's nest the female cuckoo chooses. Each female cuckoo picks the same host bird every time she lays her eggs, which means that the eggs of individual cuckoos can look very different, depending on the host species chosen.

Northern lapwing (above), European cuckoo (below)

MIGRATION

Birds move around the globe in order to find more food and to avoid freezing temperatures. They navigate by using a number of different methods, including the position of the sun and stars, mental maps, and the Earth's magnetic field. While some species undertake epic journeys across vast continents, others simply move short distances to optimize their chances of survival.

Arctic terns ➤ One of the most impressive migration journeys is carried out by the Arctic tern. This incredible creature will fly further in its lifetime than any other bird, traveling an astonishing 1.5 million miles. This globe-trotter travels between its Arctic breeding grounds and the Antarctic each year, and over the course of its life could travel roughly the equivalent of four round trips to the moon.

Bar-headed geese ➤ Some migrations require spectacular feats. The bar-headed goose journeys over the mountains of the Himalayas,

reaching heights of at least 27,000 feet above sea level, making it the highest-flying bird. The distance of the migration is not long compared to some, but bar-headed geese opt for the most direct route, which involves passing Mount Everest! They have a very large heart and extremely efficient lungs, which allow them to cope with the low pressure and temperatures better than other species. They also have a type of hemoglobin (a protein that moves oxygen around the body) in their blood which is super-efficient at absorbing oxygen at high altitudes.

Arctic terns (above)

Bar-headed geese

BIRDSONG

To produce sound, birds have a unique organ in their chest called a syrinx. The air from a bird's lungs flows across the syrinx, causing a system of membranes to vibrate. Different muscles control the pitch and volume. Most birds produce two types of sound: calls that are short and simple, and long, complicated songs used to announce their territory or to attract a mate. These songs make up the dawn chorus, which is one of the most magical sounds in nature. Different species can be distinguished by their own unique calls, and some have even been named after them, such as the kittiwake, whose call sounds like "kittee-wa-aaake," the hoopoe with its strange whooping call, and the black-capped chickadee, who sings "chick-a-dee, dee, dee."

Communication in a group ➤ Flocking birds, like starlings, rely on good communication within their group. They chatter together when roosting, bathing, and feeding so that some birds are able to forage while others keep a lookout. They have an impressive vocal range with around ten kinds of calls, all communicating different things: where they are, if there is danger around, and if they feel aggressive or agitated. Some species of bird even start to make noise while the chicks are still inside the egg! Scientists think that this might help to synchronize hatching.

Imitation ➤ Some birds are able to imitate sounds they hear around them. The Lawrence's thrush in the Amazon holds the record for imitating the largest number of species. It is known to have imitated at least 173 other Amazonian birds, as well as various frogs and insects!

The superb lyrebird in Australia has a song that is believed to be 70 percent mimicry. As well as copying the songs of those birds, it picks up human-made sounds and incorporates them into its song. These birds have been known to imitate car alarms, the click of a camera shutter, and even the sound of a chainsaw!

Starlings (left)

EXTREME COLD

On top of a mountain or out in the snow, you might not expect to find much wildlife, but there are birds who have adapted to the high altitude and freezing temperatures and have made these harsh environments their home.

High up ➤ Glaciers may not seem like the perfect place to raise a family, but they are a long way away from most predators. This is why the white-winged diuca finch, also known as the "glacier bird," has chosen to nest here. This incredible bird is the only known glacier-nesting bird, and can be found in Peru's Quelccaya Ice Cap. At more than 17,000 feet up, where temperatures at night drop to 24°F, these birds create insulated nests for their chicks to keep them safely hidden away.

Mount Everest might be the one place on earth you wouldn't expect to find any birds—but there are certain species that have even managed to conquer this mountain! The Tibetan snowcock might not be immediately visible due to its perfectly camouflaged color, but its cackle-like call often gives it away.

Camouflage ➤ Blending in superbly with the white Arctic snow is the willow ptarmigan. Only its eyes and beak give it away, as its plumage matches its surroundings perfectly. But, as the ice melts, the bird has to avoid being spotted, so it changes its plumage throughout the year. In spring, when the snow melts away, its feathers become reddish-brown to blend in with the emerging vegetation, retaining some white patches so that it can still blend in with any remaining snow. By the middle of the summer, it is a rich, brown color, again blending in with its surroundings. It then changes to a grayer color to match the fading landscape around it and then, as the winter approaches, white blotches appear as the snow starts to fall, resulting in a fully white coat once again.

White-winged diuca finch (above)

Willow ptarmigan

URBAN BIRDS

Birds are renowned for being adaptable and opportunistic, which has led to some of the bolder species setting up home in our towns and cities. Many species now thrive in urban environments, finding food and places to nest amongst bustling city life.

Once in decline, peregrine falcons are now a familiar sight in many major cities. They seek out tall buildings such as cathedrals and skyscrapers, which mimic their wild cliff habitats with suitable height and flat ledges to nest on. There is certainly no shortage of food, with the abundance of feral pigeons, as well as gulls and even bats. The peregrines sometimes hunt at night using street lights that create an orange glow over the city to help them find their prey.

Many woodland birds are moving from their traditional habitats into our urban parks. Bird trays and seed feeders provide many species, like titmice and finches, with a year-round supply of food, and these birds are also given a boost in the breeding season by the extra nest boxes and nesting material that humans often provide. But there is a downside, as our gardens also contain a number of threats, including domestic cats.

Crows and ravens maximize on our throwaway society and wastefulness. Being clever, they have figured out that they can get a free meal from a garbage can, extracting takeout containers and cartons and leaving a trail of rubbish behind.

In some Australian cities, rainbow lorikeet numbers are on the increase as the birds move away from their forest homes. The urban environment offers them an attractive place to live with plenty of food provided by wildlife-friendly gardeners. They roost in trees in large numbers for safety and often, surprisingly, in areas which are fairly well-lit, such as parking lots at shopping malls and on residential streets, so they can spot predators. These roosts, numbering up to several thousand individuals, are unpopular with many residents as they are noisy and make a considerable mess on anything that passes beneath them!

Peregrine falcon (above)